Running Toward Your Giant

By Jesse Duplantis

New Orleans, Louisiana

Unless otherwise indicated, all scripture quotations are taken from the *King James Version* of the Bible.

Running Toward Your Giant
ISBN 0-9728712-3-3
Copyright © 2003
by Jesse Duplantis

New Edition
Published by Jesse Duplantis Ministries
PO Box 1089
Destrehan, Louisiana 70047
www.jdm.org

Printed in the United States of America. All rights reserved under International Copyright Law. Contents and/or cover may not be reproduced in whole or in part in any form without express written consent of the Publisher.

Running Toward Your Giant

My mother came from a large family that always celebrated the holidays together. It still amazes me that we were all able to fit in my grandmother's small home every Thanksgiving and Christmas. As I remember those days, I can almost smell the delicious Cajun food that filled the table and taste the mouthwatering desserts stacked on the old freezer chest. But, some memories of those days are not so great.

You see, while the women were in the kitchen cooking, my dad and four uncles usually had a little entertainment planned. They loved bragging and telling tall tales about themselves, always trying to "one-up" each other with stories of strength and endurance. They also enjoyed talking about how submissive their wives were.

Of course, it was all a lot of hot air, and they knew it, but it didn't stop them from laughing and saying things like, "When I say 'jump,' my wife asks, 'how high?!'" The truth was that the men might have been the head of their house, but the women they were married to were the "necks" that could turn a hot-head around and around!

One of their favorite family sports was boxing, and the men in the family often bragged about how good their own kids could fight...which was where the entertainment came in. When my cousins and I saw the boxing gloves, all of us - girls and boys - knew that the uncles were placing bets, and we would have to fight each other again.

I remember my daddy telling my uncle, "I've got two bucks on Jesse that says he'll whip your son!" Then, my uncle would say to his son, "If you let Jesse whip you, I'll whip you too." I never ate a Christmas dinner without a swollen lip or a closed eye. Today, that is considered plain crazy and wrong, but back then, it was a different culture and time. Boxing in the front yard with your cousins was holiday family fun...at least it was fun for my uncles!

You see, although I won a few family boxing matches in my childhood, I had a girl cousin who could not be beaten. She weighed 180 pounds when she was 12 years old, and nobody messed with her — I mean nobody. I got so mad at her one time that I hit her in the head with a baseball bat. She turned toward me, looked me in the eye, and said, "You've made me mad." I knew I was in trouble.

When you stand back and look at a giant in your life, fear will arrive to try to overtake you. But, if you start running toward that giant and keep up the good fight of faith, he will fall by your side. One day you will cut his head off and show everyone how to get "a head" in life. That's what King David did when he was a young man.

Now, David wasn't what I'd call a good looking boy, but he had fierce confidence! David was ruddy faced and fair, according to 1 Samuel 17:42 and cocky enough to face a nine-foot giant without flinching. Like most teenagers, he thought he was something to be reckoned with. You know how teenage boys are. They grow one hair on their chest, and think they're a man. They blow-dry it to puff it up and make it look big. They put their mother's mascara on it and try not to sweat so it doesn't run!

David was young and thought that he was invincible because God was on his side... which is exactly how we should all be!

And the Philistine came on and drew

near unto David; and the man that bare the shield went before him.

And when the Philistine looked about, and saw David, he disdained him: for he was but a youth, and ruddy, and of a fair countenance.

And the Philistine said unto David, Am I a dog, that thou comest to me with staves? And the Philistine cursed David by his gods.

And the Philistine said to David, Come to me, and I will give thy flesh unto the fowls of the air, and to the beasts of the field.

Then said David to the Philistine, Thou comest to me with a sword, and with a spear, and with a shield: but I come to thee in the name of the LORD of hosts, the God of the armies of Israel, whom thou hast defied.

This day will the LORD deliver thee into mine hand; and I will smite thee, and take thine head from thee; and I will give the carcases of the host of the Philistines this day unto the fowls of the air, and to the wild beasts of the earth; that all the earth may know that there is a God in Israel.

And all this assembly shall know that the LORD saveth not with sword and spear: for the battle is the LORD's, and he will give you into our hands.

1 Samuel 17:41-47

Now, when David first came into the camp, his older brothers got mad at him. They belittled him because they thought he'd followed them just to see the battle. But, there was no battle to see. The entire army of Israel was hiding from Goliath and the Philistine army.

Can you imagine David's brother's reaction when he began to rebuke them and then threaten Goliath? I know they must have thought, *'What is this punk kid doing? He doesn't have any armor or weapons; all he has is a sling shot. Why is he popping off at the mouth? He's going to make that guy so mad that he'll come over here and wipe us all out!'*

The Bible says that Goliath "disdained him" because he was young and ruddy! He thought it was an insult and cursed at David, promising to feed him to the birds and the animals. But, David didn't run away from Goliath just because he was big, bad and burly; he ran *toward* him. He had an attitude that said, "You want some of me?! I'll climb up your face and rip your eyebrows out!"

David didn't care if he was small. He didn't care if he didn't have armor that fit him or a sword big enough to whip a giant. Instead, he responded to the giant's threats with words of confidence in God. *"This day will the LORD deliver thee into mine hand and I will smite thee..."* (vs. 46). Notice that David wasn't confident in his own ability but in the ability of the God he served. That's how we should be!

It doesn't matter how small or insignificant we think we are, God is big enough to fight our giant and give us the victory. We just have to be bold enough to trust Him like David and speak the end result with fierce faith.

David took the weapons he knew best, his faith and his sling-shot, and started searching the ground for stones. With that done, not only did he run toward that giant in faith, but he ran toward the entire army behind Goliath.

The Bible says that David hurled his slingshot and with a stone hit Goliath in the one spot that was unprotected - his head. *Whack!* Goliath's big body started falling to the ground, and when Goliath hit the dirt, the entire army of Israel saw it and ran toward the Philistines to defeat them.

Notice that the rest of the army gained immediate confidence after seeing the miracle of David slaying Goliath. That's what happens when one person's faith brings results. It causes others, who were once trembling in fear, to recognize the power of God and the importance of faith.

> ***It is possible to look unarmed in the estimation of men. While we fight for God, we may confidently expect that He will fight for us.***

It's amazing how many people are like David's brothers and the army of Israel. It's amazing how many who have the potential to be a "David" will stand back and let a stinking demon from hell defy the promises of God.

If you have cancer, high blood pressure, heart disease, diabetes or family or financial problems, begin to realize that the battle is not yours. It's the Lord's. You are David, and that sickness is Goliath. It is the devil's way of trying to intimidate you, destroy your confidence, and rob you of a good life.

It's time to stand up like a cocky teenager and say to that problem, "I've had enough! This day you shall bow your head at the power of Jesus in me."

I've done a little boxing in my life, and my coach used to tell me, "Boy, don't ever back up; just go forward." Sometimes your nose is bleeding, your teeth hurt and your lips feel like they could go around your head two or three times, but you can still win if you don't back up.

If you have a giant in your life, refuse to back up. It is time to run toward that problem and solve it in the power of the Holy Spirit. The world may say that you can't win your battle, but when you stand for God, He will fight for you. You can "float like a butterfly and sting like a bee" as you run toward your giant and behead it.

Sometimes I've looked at situations and thought, *'Lord I'm nothing but a ruddy-faced kid.'* That's when the power of the Holy Spirit rises within me and says, *'Don't allow that situation to defy the promises of God. Run toward that problem and defeat it in the name of Jesus!'*

When I began my television ministry, people told me that I couldn't raise the finances to pay in advance for a whole year of broadcasting. Well, I want to make an announcement: That was a big financial giant, but we looked at it and cut the giant's head off! Today, every television station that we are on is paid for in advance. We decided to go forward with a slingshot called the Holy Ghost. Glory to God!

I made a commitment not to let a financial devil destroy me. I may be smaller than everything he has against me and unarmed in the estimation of the world, but if I confidently fight for God, He shall fight for me.

Running toward your giant does not decrease its size, but rather it enables your faith to increase toward your obstacle.

Faith is like a central air thermostat on the wall. If you set a thermostat on 68 degrees, a big old unit outside will work continually, pumping cold air until the house is 68 degrees. Although that thermostat is tiny, it is so powerful that it will burn up that big unit outside before allowing it to quit. That big unit will sweat and complain, 'Hey, don't work me so hard!' But, that unyielding thermostat says, 'You will get this place cool now, or you will cease to exist!'

In the same way, faith will burn up everything in its path that tries to hinder the promises of God.

I have set my faith thermostat on high when it comes to healing. I've had to because I travel all over the country, and I am in different climates all the time. I might be cold one day and sweating the next. I may fly out of snow in Canada and arrive in Miami with humidity so thick you could cut it with a knife. I must trust God to keep me in divine health. I don't have time to get sick. There is a lost and dying world that needs to hear the Good News of Jesus Christ.

When you run toward your giant, your giant will run from you.

The first time I went to New York City, I flew into Kennedy International Airport. It was prearranged that someone from the church would be picking me up, but no one showed up. I tried to call the pastor, but he had a private telephone number, and the operator would not give it to me.

She told me that she could not give out private telephone numbers unless it was an emergency. I said, "Lady, let me ask you something? If it were your first time in New York City in Kennedy Airport and a bunch of strange people were looking at you, would you call that an emergency?" She thought a minute and said, "I'll put you through." What I did is called running toward your giant.

When my daughter was a teenager, she didn't worry about anything! Why? Because her daddy was taking care of everything. Because I was supplying all of her needs. If she encountered a giant, she gave it to me. If her car was empty, she gave it to me!

I often wondered, *Why is the car always on empty when I need to use it? Why can't I drive the car when it is full of gas?* Whenever I got in my daughter's car, I had to trust God to get me to the gas station! I was riding on fumes. Then, I'd reason, *I guess I'm the El Sha-Dad! I'm the dad who's more than enough.* I decided that if there was a giant around, I'd have to take care of it!

It's all right if you want to laugh at my situation. Laughter is good. *"A merry heart doeth good like a medicine"* (Prov. 17:22). When you laugh at your giant, it runs from you. Laughter opens up the heart. Hearing the Word brings faith. Put them together, and it's a good way to receive what you need from God. When you're doubt-free and ready, all you'll have to do is say, "Jesus," and you will receive your healing.

Some people criticize my humor, but I know exactly what I'm doing! I'm running toward some giants! I'm running with the joy of the Lord and a message of faith from

God's Word. Some people think I'm just making jokes, but I know that joy is a part of God's Spirit, and I wouldn't run towards a giant without it!

I've made up my mind that I'm going to complete my destiny in God. I don't care if it takes 30 days or 30 years, I shall finish my course with joy. God has given me a ministry, and it must be fulfilled according to His will. Do I have problems? Yes! There are many giants that pop up their ugly heads. Does it bother me? No! I've found that anytime a person does something for God, they will encounter resistance. I'm no exception!

How can I have joy even when a big problem is staring me in the face? Because I know in Whom I have believed! God will see me through! He didn't promise me that there would never be any problems in life.

In John 16:33, Jesus said, *"In the world ye shall have tribulation..."* So, I'm not surprised when trouble rears its head. But in that verse, Jesus goes on to say, *"...but be of good cheer; I have overcome the world."* I'm encouraged to be of good cheer because Jesus overcame ALL the problems of the world, and His work on earth and at the cross has made a way for me to overcome too.

Jesus came so that I could have life and that more abundantly. (John 10:10) He died so that I might live; He took the suffering so that I might be set free. I know that no matter what is standing in my way, I am going to overcome because Jesus overcame. If I just run towards my giant, with faith in His Word and confidence in His ability to help me overcome, that problem is going to be solved! I'll cut the head off of that giant problem and give glory to God!

The unchangeable God will always do the same things in the same circumstances. Recognize that an undimmed eye, a calm heart and a steady arm will see you through.

Is the devil running toward you? How long will you let him stay in your home or your church? When will you wake up and say, "Enough is enough?!" It's time to open battle on satan's works - to fight back!

David started questioning Goliath's right to harm him when he asked the question, *"...for who is this uncircumcised Philistine, that he should defy the armies of the living*

God?" (1 Sam 17:26). In other words, 'Who is this idiot without a covenant? Does he actually think he can defy God?!' You've got to get that way with the devil too. Who does he think he is trying to attack you? You're God's child! You've been made righteous. The Creator is on your side!

Why sit and wait for the devil to attack? The moment he begins taunting you and trying to harm you, start running towards him with the force of the Word of God. Don't give the devil an inch by losing confidence. Instead, get mighty! Stand up to the attack and say, "Wait a minute, this earth belongs to me."

If you believe that everything has to bow at the name of Jesus, then you should have the guts, gall and audacity to quit talking about it and start manifesting it. Don't lay there like there is nothing you can do. You have authority. You have power. Jesus died to give it to you. Start running towards your giant.

If you have a husband who's not saved, that's a giant problem in your life. But, don't cut your husband's head off! After all, he's not really your problem; your problem is the devil that is blinding your husband's eyes to the truth.

Keep your eye on the promise. Don't fight your husband in an attempt to get him saved; fight the devil who is blinding his eyes. Use the sword of the Spirit, which is the Word of God, and don't give up praying for that man - that's running towards your giant!

Even if it looks like your husband will never get saved, realize that it's just his tough luck that he married you, because you will fight to the end for his salvation. You are fighting for him, not against him. Remember, the God in you is stronger than the emptiness in him.

God calls us to be fishers of men, and that means we have to put out some good tasting bait. Fish don't bite on something that isn't appetizing. People don't want what isn't appealing. So, it's important in soul winning that you keep God's love and joy flowing in your life.

If you're sour, the unsaved will see it, and they'll be turned off to God. Like I always say, the only Jesus some people will ever see is the Jesus in you or the Jesus in me.

If you get discouraged, go to God. Let His presence give you peace and calm your heart. He's the only One who can really do that work.

Let His Word keep your eyes focused and your mind on track. The Word will light up the path you should run. The Holy Spirit will give you scriptures to stand on that will build your confidence so that you can continue running towards your giant.

Why do we play games with the devil? Because religion has taught us to do it.

The Word is clear with truth, but the religious world is muddy and wish-washy! Notice when you read the Gospels, the religious crowd didn't like Jesus. Why? Because He didn't play their stupid games! He didn't say one thing and do another. He believed in God and His power to change people's lives for the better.

Jesus is the light of the world. He broke the power of darkness everywhere He went, and we're supposed to be followers or imitators of Him (Ephesians 5:1). As long as there is a sinner in this world, we have a destiny to complete. But, many churches in America have a Samson mentality. They are living with their enemy, and he is controlling them. Samson did not deliver Israel from the Philistines. He made them live with their enemy because he loved one of their women.

God is looking for men and women like Gideon who will stand on His Word and deliver people from their enemy. It's time to stand up like Joshua and Caleb and claim your promised land. There may be giants in the land, but you are well able to defeat them in the name of Jesus. Get confident about that.

Don't let a stinking devil from hell defy the power of God in your life. Don't let the enemy or situations steal your confidence. Remember what the cross did for you. Remember who you are now in Christ!

2 Corinthians 5:17 is a great scripture. It says, *"Therefore if any man be in Christ, he is a new creature: old things are passed away; behold, all things are become new."* The old man may have given up, but you've become a new person...and you don't have to give up or give in. Temptation comes, but you're fully able to overcome it all. God is on your side, and He can help you with the details!

Make a quality decision to stand firmly on the Word of God. The Father God made a quality decision to put His Son Jesus on the cross so that you would have the ability to tell sin and satan NO!

If your son was nailed to a cross, would you rescue him from that cruel cross? Why didn't God do that?

God gave us His best when He gave us Jesus Christ. Yet, when Jesus was on the cross and cried out to His Father, God in His righteousness chose not to be controlled by His emotions because He knew the end result. He knew the price that had to be paid, and He knew that Jesus had agreed to die for the sins of the world before the foundation of the world.

That day, God made a rational, quality decision when it came to the life of His Son, Jesus Christ. Because of the great sin that hung upon Jesus, God refused to look at Him while He hung on the cross. He had to reject Him at that moment.

Jesus cried out saying, "Father, Father why hast thou forsaken me?" and He didn't say that because He was experiencing physical pain. He said it because He was suddenly and completely separated from His Father-rejected. The sins of the entire world hung on Him, and He was utterly alone, and it was unbearable. His soul was crying out.

What was Jesus doing on the cross? He

was running towards our giant...doing what needed to be done for righteousness to reign. Even though He was fully capable of coming down off of that cross, He chose to stick with His decision, and He laid down His life for you and me.

What was God, the Father, doing while Jesus was on the cross? God was running toward His giant. It hurt Him to see man spit on Jesus and devils gnash on Him, but He was focused on winning back mankind. He was focused on making the ultimate sacrifice, even though it hurt Him to leave Jesus alone on the cross. He stuck to His decision, and let the work of redemption continue. He did it for you and for me.

Jesus took His last breath on the cross, and the scripture says He went to hell for us. But, God did not plan to leave His Son in hell. Jesus was destined to overcome! He rose from the dead on the third day, just like He said He would. His spirit reunited with His body, and Jesus came out of the tomb. It was supernatural, and it was God's way of saying, 'You did it, Son! You paid the price for the sins of the world.'

Jesus' burial wrap was left as evidence

that he rose from the dead. He left that tomb in a glorified robe of righteous light. In front of His empty tomb, an angel sat on the opened stone door and proclaimed, "He's not dead. He's ALIVE!"

As every member of Heaven looked on, Jesus walked into the portals of glory. His entrance declared to His Father and all of creation that the Lamb of God who takes away the sins of the world had been sacrificed. He had ransomed back God's most prized possession - mankind.

He took a "bucket" of His precious blood and threw it across the altar, sealing man's redemption forever. Jehovah God announced to all: "Man has become the righteousness of God. Go forth with the Good News: He has risen!" Glory to God! What Jesus did for us on the cross at Calvary was like taking a blade to satan's head - He cut it off for the world to see.

Jesus ran toward His giant - mankind's sin - and demolished it. He ran toward the giants of poverty, sickness, hate and depression and annihilated them with His precious blood. He is the great conqueror who was and is victorious over every work of the enemy.

He has made you and me more than conquerors. Why did He do it?

...That all the earth may know that there is a God in Israel.
And all this assembly shall know that the Lord saveth not with sword and spear: for the battle is the Lord's, and he will give you into our hands.

1 Samuel 17:46-47

Don't stand back and let a stinking devil from hell defy the promises of God. Stand in the strength of God, run toward that giant in your life and defeat it in the name of Jesus!

Prayer of Salvation

If you don't know Jesus as your personal Lord and Savior, I'd like to take this opportunity to pray with you. All God asks is for you to come to Him with a sincere heart and accept His plan of salvation through Jesus Christ. Right now, go to Him in prayer. Speak from your heart. The Bible says in Romans 10:9-10 that if you believe on the Lord Jesus Christ with your heart and confess it with your mouth, you will be saved. Your sins will be washed away when you accept what Jesus did for you. Pray this prayer right now:

"Lord Jesus, come into my life. Forgive me of all my sins. I believe that you are the Son of God and that you died on the cross and rose from the dead to make a way for me. Thank you for loving me enough to die for me, for thinking that I was worth it. Today, I accept you into my heart and give myself totally to you. I'm tired of living my own way, and I want to live your way. I need your help. Lord, create a clean heart in me right now and guide me from now on. I love you, Jesus, and I accept you as my Savior. You are now the Lord of my life!"

If you just prayed this prayer, Congratulations!
You're starting a new life! 2 Corinthians 5:17 says when you accept Jesus as your savior, *"Old things are passed away; behold, all things are become new."*

Friend, you have a whole new way of life to look forward to. You've been given a clean slate —you are righteous now because of what Jesus did, and nobody can take that away! You're saved and starting a brand new life in Christ.

Please write to my ministry and let us know of your decision so that we can bless you with some more information and pray for you. God bless you as you start your new life with God today.

For a free catalog of other books and
tapes by Jesse Duplantis or for
information about JDM, call or write:

Jesse Duplantis Ministries
PO Box 1089
Destrehan, LA 70047
985.764.2000 Fax 985.764.0044
or
Visit us online at:
www.jdm.org

Look for these other books by
Jesse Duplantis

Wanting a God You Can Talk To
Also available in Braille

Jambalaya for the Soul
Also available in Braille

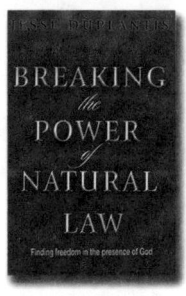

Breaking the Power of Natural Law
Also available in Braille

God Is Not Enough, He's Too Much
also available in Braille

Heaven: Close Encounters of the God Kind
also available in Braille

Look for these other books by
Jesse Duplantis

The Ministry of Cheerfulness
Also available in Braille

Heaven: Close Encounters of the God Kind
Also available in Braille or Spanish

God Is Not Enough, He's Too Much
Also available in Braille

Breaking the Power of Natural Law
Also available in Braille

Jambalaya for the Soul
Also available in Braille

Wanting a God You Can Talk To
Also available in Braille

What In Hell Do You Want?

Jesse's Mini-books

Don't Be Affected by The World's Message
The Battle of Life
Running Toward Your Giant
Keep Your Foot on The Devil's Neck
One More Night With The Frogs
Leave It In The Hands of A Specialist
The Sovereignty of God